Paper Lanterns

Elinor Brumbaugh

BookLeaf Publishing

Presentation by *BookLeaf Publishing*

Web: www.bookleafpub.com

E-mail: info@bookleafpub.com

ISBN: 9789357213950

First edition 2023

I would like to dedicate this book to all of my loved ones and friends who have passed on, yet still guide me from the other side. To my sweet mother Dottie, my uncle Jim, my great uncle Johnny, my brothers Scott and Kenny, my sister Anne Marie, my good friends Kary, Linda ("My brain hurts too!"), Chuck and Alan (You were both gold), and Andy (You lived larger than most during your short time, my friend). Life is too short. Love the people you've been blessed with while they're here to be loved.

ACKNOWLEDGEMENT

I would like to acknowledge and thank my father and brother. You are both my very best friends and confidantes - my absolute rocks. I know our connection extends many lifetimes beyond this one. I am so blessed and so, so lucky to have you both in my life. I love you guys.

I would also like to thank my friends and coworkers for the beauty, blessings and insights they bring me everyday - Chelsey Burden, Siena Litrell, Kayla Johnson, Barbara Tait, Sarah Weatherby, Sarah Andrews, Tamara Guillory, Lauran McMillan, Alex Wittenberg, Dee Hoagland, Mandy Tadder, Shea McCall, Maria Divina, Kelly Poe Wilson, Tamara Seaton, Teresa Huerena, Jess Madson, Nick Rullman, and Matt Kies. You are all incredible people who I'm so incredibly lucky to know and learn from. I love you all.

PREFACE

A series of philosophical questions and reflections posed as a small collection poems.

The Road Ahead

My head and heart
Are heavy
With tasks and trivialities
Endless inanities
As time wends its way
Ever forward
Never back
Twisting suffocating knots
Deep inside my memory
That destroy tissue
where soft cells of time reside
Now dissipating and sloughing
Silently into the ether

Enough

When will it be enough?
Enough outrage
Enough violence
Enough injustice
To push us out of
Our plodding acceptance
And into desperate action

And once we have been catalyzed
Into forward malcontent motion
Will it be too late?
Or will there be time enough?

Sight Unseen

3

The journey of
A thousand miles
Begins with unspoken trust
The sacred belief
That each quavering step
Carries the voyager
Into infinite
And unbound potential

Echoes of Cosmos

How very much
Words on the page
Seem to resemble the light of
Small winking stars
Telegraphing distant thoughts
Into a darkened firmament
Their creator just
A faint memory
An echo
Lost to the surety of time

Memento Mori

5

Remember
Each day
More sacred
Than the last
Each day
A covenant
With the Universe
A holy gift
To say I am here
To say I am aware
To say
I am

Strength

6

To breathe through
The discomfort and fear
Knowing that
After all has been done
And said
You will catch yourself in the end
Cradled in the softness
Of your own
Strength

Heavy

Sometimes
The world feels
So
Damn
Heavy
Nothing seems to alleviate,
Ameliorate or
Soothe the pain.
What substance
Elixir or potion
Can ease an
Aching soul?
Or unburden
A sorrowful heart
Awash in
The sadness of the world?
But then there is the sound of
Children's laughter -
Pure happiness and unbridled joy
And birdsongs -
Their small foreign hymns
To trees and grass and wind
And ocean waves
Murmuring gently against the shore
Or the feeling of sunshine

Soft and warm on my skin
Honied light expanding every pore
When life is overwhelming
And feels too heavy to bear
Remember the small solaces
And that little things
Are always larger
Than they seem
Drink them in
With your thirsty soul
And remember that without
Heavy
We would never know
Light

Signs

Is my time
Denoted by
A halo around
The moon?
A red sky at night?
What signifier,
What sign
Do I look for?
When do you know
It's your time
to say, "enough"
To move on and
Away from
Safety
Away from
Comfort
And to step forward
Into the exciting unknown?

Persistence

If you fall
Don't be content
To remain
Lying in the dust
Gently lift yourself up

Remember that
You too deserve every happiness
And every dream

So do not let
Your dreams die
Stillborn in your heart
Let them be born
And brought to
Blindingly brilliant life

Now

Sometimes
I forget that
All that I have
And all that I can count on
Is this very moment

I must remember
To cradle
Every sacred second
In an embrace
Of gratitude

The Cost

It is important
To remember
The exchange of
Bodily currency -
Of limbs,
Vision,
And energy
The price we pay
For golden moments
Laughing in
Amber sun

It is worth
The cost

Saying "Yes"

Oftentimes in life
Saying "yes"
Can feel like
Cold sweat and
Clammy hands
A murmuration of the heart
And sometimes even
A cessation
Of the heart's frantic scrabbling
Against it's fragile ivory cage
These seemingly ominous signals
Are not to be construed with
Signs of impending doom
But should be viewed
As harbingers of potential
Limitless
And neither
Inherently good
Or bad
But pregnant with possibility

Below

14

Silent protest
Or slow suicide?
Self medicating
Muffled cries for help
I feel nothing
I feel everything
Wave upon
Wave
Upon wave
Everything is
Overwhelm
I slowly sink
Below the abyssal surface

Fire Seed

15

I collapse inwards
A dying star
The phoenix extinguished
Unaware
That despite
My soul's seeming death
Lies a greater rebirth
A seed
Revealed by fire

Home

Each step
In perceived silence
And solitude
Is never truly alone.
All of our ancestors,
The souls departed
And spirits of loved ones
Guide us
Along the path
Leading us
Home

Time

Biological scaffolding
Our physical senses
A paltry means,
A flimsy paddle
With which to navigate
And row through
Existence
But never to
Fully understand
The complexity
Of our universe
We are hobbled
By biological
Constraints

Vanishing

My soul grows tired
Of endless streams
Of callous, thoughtless words
Of senseless acts
Selfish behavior
Barbs to the soul
Glass shards to the heart
At the expense
Of kindness
Softness
And gentleness
Loyalty
Devotion
And love
The very things
That sustain us
Vanishing before our eyes

Trapped Inside

It's like suffering at the hands of
An invisible conqueror,
An ice-colored Alexander,
An airy Attila

It's like a fly floundering in a sticky grave,
Small hair-thin legs caught fast,
Teardrop wings beating sorrowfully against
A flypaper fate

It's like the white, dying sun before the break of
winter
Trees cry red, brown, and golden tears,
As the wind mourns the dying star
With a keening whistle
Heard by fields of flowers
Nodding their heads at one another
As if to say, "what a pity, what a shame"

It's like fighting for each painful breath
As you slowly suffocate beneath a frozen lake
Your hands slip helplessly across the burning
ice,
Your consciousness swirls like wind-blown
snow
Softly into the night

Sometimes it's like you're the only mime on
earth
And you're screaming into your box of hands
Your painted face runs with emotion as people
stop to stare at you -
The latest addition to the human zoo

It's like life is a movie, and you're the only one
in the audience
You're bound to your plush luxury cinema seat
With chains you wove out of everything cold
You stare enviously as the faces chase each other
Purposefully across the screen

It's like an archaic insect
Surrounded by an amber tomb,
watching with dead eyes as years replace years
Sentenced to stay stationary for eternity
In a golden gemstone cage -
Safe, shining, and dead

To Sleep

We all succumb
To the succubus of
The rich and decadent night
Pregnant with shards
Of dark starlight -
Dark, amber fire
A heady mead
To chill the soul

First embers of the day
Burn away the hungry darkness.
Another day has come
Full of good intentions,
Like an abusive lover
As he tends to the marks
He gifted your soft flesh

One moment in sunshine,
And the next
Swinging on a rope,
Noose biting around
Your clammy flesh where
You tread the air,
As angels do

Isis and Osiris

Her gentle feathers
Sooth his flayed flesh,
Even in death
He looks upon her lovingly

His body is shrouded in moonlight,
She leans in with a vital kiss
To revive desiccated skin

Like a mother watching her child
When in sleep's callous hands
She gazes anxiously,
Checking for the soft hidden rhythms of life -
A blessed inflation of the breast

Long forgotten moments lay stranded
Like segmented pieces of his corpse
As they are ushered down the river Nile
By rapids and stately crocodiles

On wings falling like snow in the desert
She collects broken remnants,
Leaving moon-filled tears
In the stead of her lover's flesh
Winking down the Nile

Now she waits patiently
A smile alights precariously on her face
As she tends to the invisible scars
She mended with moonshine
And memory

I Remember

24

I remember
My mother's gentle voice
And the whirr of the angry washing machine
As she hung clothes out
With the clouds to dry -

Clouds chased by lonely crows who sang,
"Birds of a feather
Should trace the heavens together"
And the clothes watched
With jealous eyes

www.ingramcontent.com/pod-product-compliance
Lightning Source LLC
La Vergne TN
LVHW051247200726
843510LV00011B/1722